The HIDDEN TREASURE

Why Settle for Temporary Pleasures
When You Can Have the Eternal Treasure

DELON L. TURPIN

Treasure Trove

treas·ure trove /ˈtreZHər ˌtrōv/

A valuable discovery, resource, or collection.

Merriam-Webster Dictionary

DEDICATION

First and foremost, I dedicate this book to my Lord and Savior, Jesus Christ, who shined His magnificent light into my heart and has transformed me from the inside out. Without Your love drawing me near, I would still be left in the dark. Thank you for allowing me to be a vessel that You would use to birth this book into the earth. Thank you for loving me unconditionally.

I dedicate this book to my mom, Jacklyn, who has always been on my team. You have always been right there, cheering me on through all that I have been through. You are a wonderful example of Jesus' steadfast love, and I am grateful for your love, prayers, and support. To my brothers, my niece and nephews, my family, and friends. I pray that you experience the love of Christ through the pages of this book. May you capture the vision and run with it. Thank you for your continual prayers, love, and support.

I dedicate this book to all those who would read this book one day. I pray the Lord would reveal Himself to you in such a way that you are totally convinced of His love for you. May this book find you with an open heart, ready to receive all that God has for you. Each page is written with you in mind, and I pray that you have an encounter with the One, True, Living God, Jesus.

TREASURE TROVES

Introduction

*"But if our **gospel** be hid, it is **hid to them that are lost**: In whom **the god of this world hath blinded the minds of them which believe not**, lest **the light of the glorious gospel of Christ**, who is the image of God, should **shine unto them**. For **we preach** not ourselves, but **Christ Jesus the Lord**; and ourselves your servants for Jesus' sake. For **God**, who **commanded the light to shine out of darkness**, hath **shined in our hearts, to give the light of the knowledge of the glory of God in the face of Jesus Christ**. But **we have this treasure in earthen vessels**, that **the excellency of the power may be of God, and not of us***" (2 Corinthians 4:3-7 KJV).

My sole intent in writing this book is even if one life is impacted and turned towards the Kingdom of God, He will ultimately get all the glory. I pray what is written between the covers of this book will bless you whether you are a new believer in Jesus Christ, already are a believer but have lost your way, or maybe you have not yet come to know Him. God is beckoning us to go deeper and draw nearer to Him. We may not sense it sometimes because we often allow the cares of this world to speak louder to us than His still small voice that whispers within. Yet, this space in our hearts longs for something that can only be filled with the love of God, and there comes a time when the gospel (the good news) of salvation is heard, and you are aware that you can no longer ignore it, but a choice must be made. Will you accept His invitation or dismiss it? Will you get another opportunity?

You may wonder why the title "The Hidden Treasure." As you read this book, I hope you discover this invaluable treasure. So many times, we tend to seek after worldly pleasures, not realizing there is an Eternal Treasure who is far greater than anything the world can offer. According to 2 Corinthians 4:18 (NIV), we must fix our eyes not on what is seen but on what is unseen, since what is seen is temporary, but what is unseen is eternal.

Proverbs 25:2 (KJV) states that it is the glory of God to conceal a thing: but the honor of kings is to search out a matter. What if you knew there was a hidden treasure somewhere waiting for you? The first vision you may have would be of a treasure chest filled with gold, silver, and various jewels in all its splendor. Maybe you would envision someone leaving you a large sum of money as an inheritance. Either way, the excitement would be difficult to contain. You would put all your effort into searching for this treasure until it was found or use every available resource to obtain it. You would be filled with so much anticipation; waiting for the day would seem like an eternity. But what if I tell you that this treasure far exceeds any expectation, outweighs any exorbitant amount of money, and is worth more than any tangible item, and yet is closer than you can imagine.

Jesus taught the disciples, His followers, many times by speaking in parables which are short, meaningful stories that have spiritual significance. He wanted the disciples to understand what the Kingdom of Heaven was like. He described how glorious and valuable this Kingdom was and likened the Kingdom to something that a person would find to be priceless. For example, in Matthew 13:44-46 (NKJV), He says that the Kingdom of Heaven is like a treasure hidden in the field, which a man found and hid again; and from joy over it, he goes and sells all that he has and buys that field.

As you begin this journey, allow the Scriptures referenced in this book to be the beginning of a lifetime of discovery. I hope you take a moment to look them up in the Bible and read the chapter that the verse is written. You may even find yourself going further. I pray you gain a greater depth of understanding as you continue to delve deeper into His Word. I believe as you continue to seek after God, you will begin to develop such an intense hunger for the Word of God, and your thirst for more of Him will be satisfied (ref. Psalm 107:9 NIV, Matthew 5:6 KJV). Let the Word be like a compass that helps you navigate along this faith walk that you are about to embark on. May you encounter the One, the Spirit of Truth, who promises to guide you into all truth (John 16:13 NIV). For God, the Father, sent the living Word, Jesus, His Son into the world as the Light of the world to illuminate the darkness in our hearts. After Jesus died on the cross and was resurrected, He sent the promised Holy Spirit to live within those who would acknowledge Jesus as Lord. In other words, He came to save the lost. Now, that is good news.

"For God so loved the world, that He gave His only Son, that whoever believes in Him should not perish but have eternal life" (John 3:16 ESV).

If you have not accepted Jesus as your Lord and Savior, but by God's divine plan, you are reading this book, I believe He is calling you to come closer. I invite you to take advantage of this opportunity to open your heart and ask Him to come into your life. Acknowledging that you need a Savior, your willingness to surrender your will and your plans in exchange for His and repent or turn from your sins is just the beginning of a new way of life. Below I have provided a prayer of salvation if you choose to accept Jesus into your heart at this time. However, if you want first to explore the many various treasures written within this book before you make this very important decision that I hope will leave you convinced that you are accepted and loved, you can return to this prayer at any time.

"If you declare or confess with your mouth Jesus is Lord and believe in your heart that God raised Him from the dead, you will be saved. For it is with your heart you believe and are justified (just as if you have never sinned), *and it is with your mouth that you profess your faith and are saved"* (Romans 10: 9-10 NIV).

Prayer of Salvation
(Read out loud)

Jesus, I come to you, maybe not with the full understanding of how this all works, but I know there must be an exchange for me to continue along this journey. I repent of my sins and ask you, Jesus, to come into my heart, reveal yourself to me, and help me to grow in my understanding. Thank you for taking on my punishment by dying on the cross, the place where your blood was shed so that all my sins would be forgiven. Thank you for paying that ultimate price. The grave could not hold you; death could not keep you because you who did not sin was able to conquer sin and death, and on the third day, you rose to sit at the right hand of God, the Father. I thank you for loving me so much that you gave your life so that I could have eternal life, and now I confess that Jesus is my Lord and Savior.

Amen.

If you have chosen to accept the gift of salvation at this time and have prayed this prayer, you are now a citizen of the Kingdom of Heaven. For it is by grace you have been saved, through faith; and this not from yourselves, it is a gift of God, not by works, so that no one can boast (Ephesians 2:8-9 NIV). Whether you are a new believer or rededicated your life to the Lord, I, along with the angels in heaven, rejoice! Yes, there is rejoicing in the presence of the angels of God over one sinner who repents (Luke 15:10 NIV). You have now begun a new journey with Jesus Christ, and you will want to find a Bible-believing church, one that believes in God the Father, God the Son, Jesus, and God the Holy Spirit, where you can learn and be discipled and taught the Word of God. The Bible says, *"In Him you also, when you heard the word of truth, the gospel of your salvation, and believed in Him, were sealed with the promised Holy Spirit, who is the guarantee of our inheritance until we acquire possession of it, to the praise of His glory"* (Ephesians 1:13-14 ESV).

The Holy Spirit is a Comforter and Helper, a friend who will walk alongside you and lead you. *"I will instruct you and teach you in the way you should go; I will counsel you with my loving eye on you"* (Psalm 32:8 NIV).

This book is unlike any other in the sense that it is written not like a normal book. It is not a novel or a devotional, and each section, which I call a Treasure Trove, not a chapter, might not necessarily follow the previous section like a usual book would read. However, each Treasure Trove will consist of a golden nugget, a hidden treasure based on the Scriptures, essentially something of value that I have learned along my journey. After completing this book, I believe you will not only have an increased desire to explore the Bible more intently, but you will also cultivate a deeper relationship with God leading you to discover His will and purpose for your life as it all comes together like a special gift, He has just for you.

"Seek first the Kingdom of God and His righteousness [His way of doing and being right- the character of God] and all these things will be given to you as well" (Matthew 6:33 NIV, [AMP]).

When you find something of immense value,

nothing else matters but securing it

because you realize

there is nothing more desirable

than to be changed literally

from the inside out.

~ Delon Turpin

TREASURE TROVE I
Matthew 25:1-13
(NLT)

1 "Then the Kingdom of Heaven will be like ten bridesmaids[a] who took their lamps and went to meet the bridegroom. 2 Five of them were foolish, and five were wise. 3 The five who were foolish didn't take enough olive oil for their lamps, 4 but the other five were wise enough to take along extra oil. 5 When the bridegroom was delayed, they all became drowsy and fell asleep.

6 "At midnight they were roused by the shout, 'Look, the bridegroom is coming! Come out and meet him!'

7 "All the bridesmaids got up and prepared their lamps. 8 Then the five foolish ones asked the others, 'Please give us some of your oil because our lamps are going out.'

9 "But the others replied, 'We don't have enough for all of us. Go to a shop and buy some for yourselves.'

10 "But while they were gone to buy oil, the bridegroom came. Then those who were ready went in with him to the marriage feast, and the door was locked. 11 Later, when the other five bridesmaids returned, they stood outside, calling, 'Lord! Lord! Open the door for us!'

12 "But he called back, 'Believe me, I don't know you!'

13 "So you, too, must keep watch! For you do not know the day or hour of my return.

Prepare for The Wedding Banquet!

Most little girls dream of and look forward to the day they say, "I Do," to the one they have chosen to marry on their wedding day. Every bride plans for that day as every groom waits with anticipation for their bride to walk down the aisle. It is safe to say that a wedding is usually well planned, and a lot of preparation and effort goes into making that day special. In Matthew 25, Jesus tells the disciples a parable of a wedding feast that ten virgins (bridesmaids) were invited to attend. Although parables were spoken to the disciples for a reason, they have been written for our benefit as well. Jesus told several parables to relay a spiritual lesson or message.

In this parable, Jesus tells of ten virgins and how there were five wise and five foolish. The virgins had a heightened expectation of meeting the bridegroom and entering the wedding feast. The wise virgins prepared themselves in advance by storing oil in their lamps; however, the foolish did not store any extra oil. At that time, lamps were kept lit using olive oil, and one end of the wick had to be submerged in the oil for the lamp to remain lit. The wise virgins were not sure when the bridegroom would arrive, but they knew that if they wanted to participate in the celebration of the wedding feast, they had to be ready. In this parable, the bridegroom is symbolic of Jesus, and the bridesmaids represent the church (the bride of Christ).

As the virgins waited for the bridegroom to arrive, they all fell asleep, and their lights began to dim. But, at midnight, there was a shout! Here is the bridegroom, come out! All the virgins awoke and had to trim their lamps (their wicks). The five wise were able to do that because they had oil stored up in their reservoir; however, the five foolish did not and said to the wise virgins, give us some of your oil, and the wise responded go and buy some for yourselves. You see, wicks were trimmed by cutting off the old, dried-out part, that which was not useful, that which hindered the flow of the oil from being drawn up from the reservoir for the light to shine brighter. The oil in the lamps represents the Holy Spirit who dwells in those who have accepted Jesus as their Lord and Savior. The lamp would then signify us, the believer.

"You are the light of the world. A city set on a hill cannot be hidden. Nor do people light a lamp and put it under a basket, but on a stand, and it gives light to all in the house" (Matthew 5:14-15 ESV). The church represents the "light," which is not supposed to fade out but is meant to burn bright to attract those who are lost and without Jesus and to illuminate dark places. Psalm 119:105 (NIV) states the Word of God is a lamp for my feet and a light on my path. Therefore, to be the light and to remain brightly lit, we must immerse ourselves in the Word and allow it not only to guide and direct us but to work in us so that we may play an integral role in helping others to find their way to Jesus.

In John 8:12 (NLT), Jesus said, "I am the Light of the world. If you follow Me, you won't have to walk in darkness because you will have the light that leads to life." We are not instructed just to read the Word, but to meditate (to ponder or think deeply) upon it, then we become like trees planted by the rivers of water, which will yield fruit in season, and our leaves also shall not wither and whatever we do shall prosper (ref. Psalm 1:2-3 KJV). As you get understanding, the Word begins to work its way in and through you, and eventually, you begin to exude the character of God. Scripture tells us, *"But the Holy Spirit produces this kind of fruit in our lives: love, joy, peace, patience, kindness, goodness, faithfulness, gentleness, and self-control"* (Galatians 5:22-23 NLT).

After hearing the call, the announcement, the virgins who were prepared and had oil in their lamps (reservoir) were able to enter the wedding banquet, and upon entering, the door was shut. After the foolish virgins went away to buy some oil, they returned only to find the door shut. Knocking on it, they said, Lord, Lord open the door for us. His response was, "Truly I tell you; I don't know you." To think how they felt after hearing that must have crushed them beyond imagination. Now, does that compel you to get ready and be prepared for His return?

Can you imagine waiting with such expectancy for someone to let you into a ceremony only to be told I don't know who you are?

As His children, we prepare ourselves by seeking God, meditating on His Word, praying, and cultivating a relationship with Him by relying on the Holy Spirit. In the following treasure troves, you will learn of several ways you can keep your light lit.

"And the angel said to me, "Write this; Blessed are those who are invited to the wedding feast of the Lamb." And He added, "These are the true words that come from God" (Revelation 19:9 NLT).

A moment to reflect...

TREASURE TROVE II

Exodus 7:16
(NLT)

Then announce to him, 'The Lord, the God of the Hebrews, has sent me to tell you, "Let my people go, so they can worship me in the wilderness." Until now, you have refused to listen to him.

Worship in The Wilderness

The book of Exodus is about the deliverance of God's people, the Israelites, and Him fulfilling the promise He made to Abraham. It was God's plan from the beginning to establish a people with whom He could have a relationship and call his own. After raising up Moses, whom He would call to deliver his people through a wondrous display of signs and wonders, God would repeatedly have Moses say to Pharoah (the ruler of Egypt), "The Lord, the God of the Hebrews, has sent me to say to you: Let my people go, so that they may worship me in the wilderness."

Why would the Lord want His people to be set free from bondage to worship Him in the wilderness? One thing I have realized is that you can't freely worship God if you are still in bondage to something or someone else. In the case of the Israelites, although God delivered them from Egyptian slavery, they still had the same mentality by being immersed in that culture for over 400 years. You would think with all the signs and wonders God demonstrated by sending the ten plagues and the parting of the Red Sea;

the Israelites would have no problem believing God. However, because of their disobedience, unbelief, constant murmuring and complaining, and looking back to the past at how their lives were in Egypt, they rebelled and resorted to worshipping idols or graven images and not the One, True, Living God. This led them to wander in the wilderness for 40 years when the journey should have only taken 11 days. God wanted His people to realize that He was their God, their one and only source, the One who would provide all that they would need. Like the Israelites, it is God's desire to deliver us from bondage. The Bible says, if the Son sets you free, you will be free indeed (John 8:36 NIV). We have a responsibility to gain a deeper understanding and allow God to open our eyes and touch our hearts as we seek after Him. If we do not, we have the same tendency to want to return to the familiar. In Exodus 13:17-18 (NIV), the Bible says when Pharoah let the people go, God did not lead them on the road through the Philistine country, though it was shorter. For God said, "If they face war, they might change their minds and return or retreat back to Egypt." So, God led the people in a roundabout way through the wilderness toward the Red Sea. Thus, the Israelites left Egypt like an army ready for battle." I encourage you to read the full story in Exodus if you are not familiar with it.

Just as it was back then, the wilderness can be a season of great testing, temptation, and trials, but also a time where God's character is revealed. Challenges present great opportunities for us to get to know God more intimately because they cause us to lean and depend on Him for guidance and to trust Him in every situation. It is during these times that we learn to walk by faith and not by sight (living our lives in a manner consistent with our confident belief in God's promises) (2 Corinthians 5:7 AMP). We discover how great His faithfulness is towards us, that His love is extravagant, His grace (unmerited or undeserved favor) is sufficient, and His tender mercies (compassion or forgiveness) are new every morning. It is in the wilderness seasons of our lives that we find Him to be our Healer, our Provider, our Protector, our Peace, our Deliverer, I could keep going, but in essence, He is all that we need. It is a time where we, as His children, learn not only who He is in us but who we are in Him. There are several examples of those who went through "wilderness experiences" in the Bible, including Jesus Himself. As a matter of fact, after Jesus was baptized in the Jordan river, the Bible states in Luke 4, filled with the Holy Spirit, He was led by the Holy Spirit into the wilderness to be tempted by the devil. After a period of 40 days and nights without food, when Jesus was most susceptible to attack, the devil came to tempt and test Him and challenge His identity by trying to get Jesus to worship him. However, with each temptation, Jesus spoke with such authority the written Word of God that the devil had to ultimately leave Him, as the Bible states, until an opportune time. After this time, Jesus left the wilderness in the power of the Holy Spirit.

When we think of worship, we may envision hands lifted as we sing to an audience of One, and yes, that is one form of expression which I love to incorporate when I spend time in God's presence. To worship God is a posture of humility when you cannot help but bow in adoration and recognize He is God, and besides Him, there is no other god. He is the King of all kings and the Lord of lords. To worship God is to acknowledge Him in all that you do and say, to reverence Him, to speak well of Him, and to ascribe to Him the glory, honor, and praise that is due His name. Psalm 100:1-4 (NIV) says that we should worship the Lord with gladness; come before him with joyful songs. Know that the Lord is God. It is He who made us, and we are His; we are His people, the sheep of His pasture. Enter His gates with thanksgiving and His courts with praise; give thanks to Him and praise His name. Worship, thanksgiving, and praise are essential to ushering in the presence of God. It is imperative for your spiritual development that you create an environment that is conducive and welcoming of His holy presence. You can do this by saturating the atmosphere with praise and worship, whether in the form of worship music or singing songs that serve as a reminder of who He is, all the while thanking Him for what He has done. This is one sure way to keep the devil at bay because he cannot stand to be in the same place where we are giving God the glory. Scripture tells us in Psalm 22:3 (KJV) that God inhabits the praises of His people. In other words, God occupies or settles in an atmosphere full of worship and praise.

As I have stated previously, God's plan when He created us was to have a relationship with us. Relationships always begin with a decision and a mutual desire between two people who put forth the effort to communicate and learn from each other. God longs for you to commune with Him through prayer. This is how you establish an intimate relationship with the Father and learn how deep His unconditional love is for you, and He, in turn, reveals who you are and what He has created you to do. As the Lord said to the Israelites, I have loved you with an everlasting love; I have drawn you with unfailing kindness, so He says the same to you Jeremiah 31:3 (NIV). A relationship must be built on a foundation of trust. There is no one greater than Jesus, our Rock, to begin the process of establishing a relationship.

When you find yourself in the middle of the wilderness facing trials and tests of your own, many times, you will be faced with a choice whether you will continue to walk by faith (belief without seeing in the natural) or will you compromise and walk by what you see. Now faith, according to Hebrews 11:1(KJV), is the substance of things hoped for, the evidence of things not seen, and the sixth verse goes on to say, but without faith, it is impossible to please Him: for he that cometh to God must believe that He is and that He is a rewarder of them that diligently seek Him. The enemy, more commonly known as the devil, is now angry that you made the decision to join the kingdom of God, and he will do everything in his power to steal from you and try to deter you from ever reaching your divine purpose in Christ. According to John 10:10 (ESV), Jesus says, "The thief comes only to steal, kill, and destroy; I came that they may have life, and have it abundantly." He will set up traps and temptations in hopes that you will bite the bait so that you will be led by your flesh and not by the Spirit of God. The devil is a thief and a liar, and his goal is to lead you to your demise so that God does not get any glory out of your life. I am not saying this to instill fear in you, but to help you understand that the enemy is real, and now that you have chosen the winning side with Jesus, the devil will do whatever it takes to stunt your spiritual growth. Remember, "...greater is He that is in you than he who is in the world" (1 John 4:4 KJV). The devil does not want you to get an understanding of God's Word because then he knows you become a worthy and formidable opponent. He wants you to remain blind and not get the revelation of who Jesus is and what He has done for you. Proverbs 4:7 (KJV) says, wisdom is the principal thing; therefore, get wisdom: and with all thy getting, get understanding.

As was stated above, it is in the wilderness seasons that we find ourselves either submitting to God and digging deeper into His Word, or we succumb to the enemies' devices and are led astray. As a child of God, we have His Spirit on the inside of us, and as we grow and learn to submit to God and resist the devil, the Bible says that he will flee (ref. James 4:7 NIV). The keyword in that Scripture is that we must first submit or surrender to God. No one is perfect, and yes, it is inevitable that we all make mistakes in life, I can attest, but just like we grow in the natural from the infancy stage to adulthood, so it is with spiritual development that there comes a time where the cycle of making the same mistake must be broken, and we do an about-face and turn to God and begin to do what is right. This is called repentance. Repentance is a gift from God and is key to maintaining your relationship with Him. You are, in essence, asking God for forgiveness and turning towards Him for His help. 1 John 1:9 (ESV) states if we confess our sins to Him, He is faithful and just to forgive us our sins and to cleanse us from all unrighteousness. The Bible says, *"for all have sinned and fall short of the glory of God, and all are justified freely by His grace through the redemption that came by Christ Jesus"* (Romans 3:23-24 NIV). Repentance is like taking a shower in His grace and mercy and allowing the blood that Jesus shed for us to cleanse us from all the impurities and toxic pollutants that try to attach to us every day. King David is a perfect example of a man who sinned but returned to God in repentance and worshiped in the wilderness. Even though David knew the Lord intimately, he also gave in to temptation by committing adultery with Uriah's wife Bathsheba and eventually having Uriah killed by placing him on the frontlines in battle 2 Samuel 11 (NIV). So, when we read Scriptures that David penned, like Psalm 51, we get a sense of the pain and remorse he felt for the wrong he had done, what he did to rectify it, and as a result, the Lord saw fit to restore their relationship. Attached to sin are consequences, and according to Romans 6:23 (NIV), the wages of sin is death, but the gift of God is eternal life in Christ Jesus our Lord.

During this season of our lives, we learn about who we are in Christ, that is, if we allow Him into those hidden areas, you know those private areas we like to keep between "me, myself and I." God knows and sees all, so we cannot hide. We find that God is the only one who we can trust with our character flaws as well as with the issues of our hearts. He is our Creator, and He wants us to let Him into all the areas, the good, the bad, and the ugly, as He cares for us. When you recite Psalm 139:23-24, you are in essence inviting the Holy Spirit to come into every hidden place to search you and to know your heart, to test you and know your anxious thoughts and point out any wickedness (selfishness, pride, greed, jealousy, etc.) in you, and lead you in the way everlasting. Issues that you thought were hidden begin to come to the surface for you to address and if you give them over to God, He, in turn, will allow more and more of His light to shine in and through you.

Why "worship" in the wilderness? When we learn to worship God in the wilderness seasons of our lives, we are essentially saying to Him, no matter what, I trust you. One of the first Scriptures I put to memory when I accepted Christ was, *Trust in the Lord with all your heart and lean not on your own understanding; in all your ways acknowledge or submit to Him, and He shall direct your paths"* (Proverbs 3:5-6 NKJV).

When we worship God, we are putting Him first and above all else, even our flesh. Just as I alluded to earlier, during the infancy stage, as a baby crawls before they walk and as they start off drinking milk and eventually grow to consume more substantial food, it is with us as we develop spiritually, we begin to incorporate spiritual food and initiate spiritual disciplines such as prayer and fasting, praise and worship and the study of God's Word in our daily regimen. Reading and doing what the Word instructs is like food for our souls; we become stronger, and before long, we find our-selves overcoming obstacles or conquering bad habits that could have led us on a downward spiral. Worshipping God in the wil-derness, acknowledging Him through every trial, and depending on Him, helps us to keep our focus upon Him as He brings us through every challenge victoriously.

To sum it up, when you find yourself in the wilderness, re-member what Jesus has already accomplished for you on the cross; He has purchased your freedom and has given you the victory in Him no matter what test, trial, or temptation you find yourself fac-ing. It is inevitable that we will find ourselves in the wilderness at some point along our journey, but it is what we do and who we become during this time that will determine whether we move for-ward or go around the same mountain.

A moment to reflect...

TREASURE TROVE III

Psalm 16:11
(ESV)

You make known to me the path of life; in your presence there is fullness of joy; at your right hand are pleasures forevermore.

In His Presence is His Provision

God desires so much for His children to dwell in His presence. This place is often referred to as His dwelling place or secret place where His glory is evident. A place that He calls us to come and drink from a well in Him that promises to quench our thirsty souls. It has always been the heart of the Father to be in the midst of His people. In the ancient days of Moses and the Israelites, the Lord wanted them to know that He was always nearby and that He would not leave them. So, as they continued to make the trek towards the promised land, *"By day the Lord went ahead of them in a pillar of cloud to guide them on their way and by night in a pillar of fire to give them light, so that they could travel by day or night. Neither the pillar of cloud by day nor the pillar of fire by night left its place in front of the people"* (Exodus 13:21-22 NIV).

The Lord gave Moses specific instructions on how to construct the "Tabernacle," a meeting place so that His presence, His glory cloud, would go wherever they traveled and descend when God wanted to speak to His people. Solomon would later build the Temple in Jerusalem. Within the innermost part of the Tabernacle and the Temple was the "Holy of Holies" that housed the Ark of the Covenant, which was symbolic of the presence of God. It represented not only God's presence but His promise to defend and protect His people. Once a year, a designated High Priest would enter the "Holy of Holies" or "The Most Holy Place," and it was his responsibility to present a sin offering to God that was without blemish on behalf of the people and himself. Both the High Priest and the sacrifice had to be in accordance with the holy standards of God to be acceptable. There was a veil that separated the people from the presence of God, but after Jesus was crucified on the cross, the Bible says in Matthew 27:51 (NKJV) that the veil of the temple was torn from top to bottom. Jesus was the only one who lived a sinless life and, therefore, was the only one who could satisfy the requirement once and for all. He paid a price that we could not pay by shedding His blood on the cross and became that sacrificial Lamb who was slain so that our sins would be forgiven. This allowed us access to God's presence so that no matter what day or time it is, we can approach our loving Father and commune with Him directly through the Holy Spirit. Now our bodies, these earthen vessels, are the temples that house His precious Holy Spirit. This was God's intent all along. Hebrews 10:19-22 (AMP) says that as believers, we have the confidence to enter the Holy Place by the blood of Jesus, by this new and living way which He opened for us through the veil, that is, through His flesh, and since we have a great Priest over the house of God, let us approach God with a sincere heart and with the full assurance that faith brings, having had our hearts sprinkled clean from an evil conscience, and our bodies washed with pure water.

It is imperative that you see throughout Scripture God promised not to leave His people alone, a promise that also pertains to us. In Genesis 28:15 (NIV), God spoke to Jacob in a dream reminding him of a promise He made to his father Abraham, that He would give him descendants that would span throughout the earth and his offspring would be blessed. God said that He would be with him and would watch over him wherever he went and would not leave him until what He promised to do was done. Again, the Lord would speak to Joshua after the death of Moses, "as I was with Moses, so will I be with you; I will never leave you nor forsake you" (Joshua 1:5 NIV). As was spoken to the people of old, Jesus also speaks to His bride, the church today. In Matthew 28:20 (NKJV), after He commissioned the church to go and make disciples of all nations, He reassures us that He would be with us always, even to the end of the age.

During Jesus' ministry on earth, He would often confront people who worshipped other gods, carved images that were man-made, that could not breathe, speak, or move, and yet it was the object of choice to worship for so many at that time and even now. Idol worship has been an issue since the beginning of time because the creation or object is worshipped above the one who created it, the Creator, God, Elohim. It was and still is so prevalent through-out the world. This is so crucial to address because many are un-aware that Jesus, who walked the earth, died, and was resurrected, is the one and only, True, Living God. There is no stone, rock, or statue that has healing power or can provide for all your needs. There is, however, only one God, one Healer, one Provider who can, and His name is Jesus. We were not created to substitute one god for another or put anything in the place that is only designated for God. Many times, we can idolize money, relationships, success, and any other thing that we prioritize above God. He doesn't want a part of you but all of you as He calls you to a place of surrender. Surrender your ways for His way and your will for His will.

According to Romans 12:1 (NIV), We are to offer our bodies as a living sacrifice, holy and pleasing to God – for this is our true and proper worship.

In Acts 17:16-34 (NLT), we see the Apostle Paul travels to Athens, where Scripture tells us he is deeply troubled to see that the city was full of idols. In the synagogue, he reasoned with the Jews and God-fearing Gentiles and spoke to whoever was present. There were some who questioned and mocked him and would start a debate with him because he spoke about Jesus and his resurrection. They could not understand the new teaching that was being preached, but they wanted to know more about it.

"So Paul, standing before the council, addressed them as follows: "Men of Athens, I notice that you are very religious in every way, for as I was walking along I saw your many shrines. And one of your altars had this inscription on it: 'To an Unknown God.' This God, whom you worship without knowing, is the one I'm telling you about.

"He is the God who made the world and everything in it. Since he is Lord of heaven and earth, he doesn't live in man-made temples, and human hands can't serve his needs—for he has no needs. He himself gives life and breath to everything, and he satisfies every need. From one man he created all the nations throughout the whole earth. He decided beforehand when they should rise and fall, and he determined their boundaries.

"His purpose was for the nations to seek after God and perhaps feel their way toward him and find him—though he is not far from any one of us. For in him we live and move and exist. As some of your own poets have said, 'We are his offspring.' And since this is true, we shouldn't think of God as an idol designed by craftsmen from gold or silver or stone.

"God overlooked people's ignorance about these things in earlier times, but now he commands everyone everywhere to repent of their sins

and turn to him. For he has set a day for judging the world with justice by the man he has appointed, and he proved to everyone who this is by raising him from the dead" (Acts 17:22-31 NLT).

Previously, I had mentioned that we enter His presence with praise, worship, a heart of gratitude, and a repentant spirit. According to Psalm 51:17 (NLT), the sacrifice God desires is a broken spirit. He does not reject a broken and repentant heart. Oftentimes, it is when we accept His invitation just to set aside time and space to sit at the feet of Jesus and just be present in His presence, to behold Him and worship Him in the beauty, or splendor, of His holiness Psalm 96:9 (NIV), that we sense His peace in the midst of chaos. To behold Him is to gaze upon or fix your eyes upon Him. He is our "MasterPeace." To become who we are in Him, we must behold who He is in us. When we begin to rest in Him and wait patiently for Him, we find Him. He has always been there, but we may not have quieted the noise within to hear His voice. He is always speaking, but we must take the time to listen. He wants us to seek Him. According to Isaiah 55:6 (NIV), we are told to seek the Lord while He may be found; call on Him while He is near. Jeremiah 29:13 (NIV) the Lord says, You will seek me and find me when you seek me with all your heart. He wants to be involved in every aspect of our lives, and as we diligently seek Him, He rewards us Hebrews 11:6 (ESV). So, I encourage you to get to know the heart of the Father, enter into His presence, and receive all that He has for you. Be like David, who was a man after God's own heart, who desired God's presence and wrote, *"My heart says of you, "Seek His face!" Your face, Lord, I will seek"* (Psalm 27:8 NIV).

When you enter His presence, you will find that He provides everything that you could need. Below are some of the wonderful blessings that you receive in His presence.

Joy – *"In His presence there is fullness of joy"* (Psalm 16:11 ESV).

Liberty and Freedom – *"But whenever anyone turns to the Lord, the veil is taken away. Now the Lord is the Spirit, and where the Spirit of the Lord is, there is* [liberty] *freedom"* (2 Corinthians 3:16-17 NIV).

Transformation – *"So all of us who have that veil removed can see and reflect the glory of the Lord. And the Lord – who is the Spirit- makes us more and more like Him as we are changed into His glorious image"* (2 Corinthians 3:18 NLT).

Rest – *"And the Lord replied, "My presence will go with you and I will give you rest"* (Exodus 33:14 NIV).

"Come to me, all you who are weary and burdened, and I will give you rest" (Matthew 11:28 NIV).

Peace – *"I have said these things to you, that in me you may have peace. In the world you will have tribulation. But take heart; I have overcome the world"* (John 16:33 ESV).

Healing – *"God anointed Jesus of Nazareth with the Holy Ghost and with power; who went about doing good and healing all that were oppressed of the devil; for God was with Him"* (Acts 10:38 KJV).

"But I will restore you to health and heal your wounds, declares the Lord, because you are called and outcast, Zion for whom no one cares" (Jeremiah 30:17 NIV).

Restoration – *"Then you will call on me and come and pray to me, and I will listen to you. You will seek me and find me when you seek me with all your heart. I will be found by you, declares the lord, and will bring you back from captivity"* (Jeremiah 29:12-14 NIV).

Strength – *"Seek the Lord and His strength; seek His presence continually!"* (1 Chronicles 16:11 ESV)

"But the Lord stood by me and strengthened me, so that through me the message might be fully proclaimed, and all the Gentiles might hear it" (Timothy 4:17 ESV).

Safety – *"You hide them in the shelter of your presence, safe from those who conspire against them. You shelter them in your presence, far from accusing tongues"* (Psalm 31:20 NLT).

Refreshing – *"I will refresh the weary and satisfy the faint"* (Jeremiah 31:25 NIV).

Protection – *"He who dwells in the secret place of the Most High, shall abide under the shadow of the Almighty"* (Psalm 91:1 NKJV).

Grace and Mercy – *"Let us therefore come boldly to the throne of grace, that we may obtain mercy and find grace to help in time of need"* (Hebrews 4:16 NKJV).

SEEK YOUR FACE

As I begin to pray, I yearn to connect

On a deeper level, with the Holy Spirit

Asking for guidance, protection, and peace

Wisdom, knowledge and understanding

Longing to communicate with You my Lord and Savior

Giving you praise, glory and honor

Thanking You for Your unmerited favor

In Your patience You waited for me to respond to Your voice

What love You have shown me by giving me that choice

For we are sinners by nature and through faith in Jesus we are forgiven

Reborn we became a new creation

You shed Your blood on the cross and on You our sins were placed

That is why I am indebted to You and each day seek Your face.

~Delon Turpin

A moment to reflect...

TREASURE TROVE IV

2 Peter 1:4
(NLT)

And because of his glory and excellence, he has given us great and precious promises. These are the promises that enable you to share his divine nature and escape the world's corruption caused by human desires.

His Great and Precious Promises

I once heard in a sermon that there are 8,810 promises in the Bible. In the Strong's Concordance, the Greek word for promise is *epaggelia* which means a declaration, an announcement, a divine assurance of good or blessing. All of us make promises to one another every day; however, I have learned that a promise is only as good as the character of the one who makes it. When it comes to the promises that God has written for us in His Word, we can rest assured that they will come to pass. His promises give us hope and help us to press through the difficult times, and encourage us not to give up when everything around us appears contrary. Hebrews 6:12-14 (NIV, [AMP]) admonishes us not to become lazy or spiritually sluggish but to imitate those who, through faith and patience, have inherited or obtained what has been promised. For when God made the promise to Abraham, He swore [an oath] by Himself, since He had no one greater by whom to swear, saying I will surely bless you and give you many descendants.

I want you to envision this based upon Isaiah 55:11(NIV), once God makes a promise and His Word is spoken, it is sent on a divine mission, and it cannot return to Him without fulfilling that assignment or purpose which it was sent to accomplish. In 2 Corinthians 1:20, I like how it is written in the New Living Translation, For all God's promises have been fulfilled in Christ with a resounding "Yes!" And through Christ, our "Amen" (which means "Yes") ascends to God for His glory. Here we see that His promises have already been fulfilled in Christ and when our Yes comes into agreement with His Yes, then His Word must come to fruition. In Luke 1:37 (NIV), it reads that no Word from God will ever fail. I believe when you and I speak the Word of God, our faith increases. *"So then faith comes by hearing, and hearing by the word of God"* (Romans 10:17 NKJV). When you lay hold of a promise from the Bible, it is like a seedling that is planted in your heart and, when watered by faith and the spoken Word of God along with patience, eventually produces the promise in your life.

Throughout Scripture, God made promises (covenants) with His people and has never reneged on any of them. The Bible says, *"God is not a man, so He does not lie. He is not human, so He does not change his mind. Has He ever spoken and failed to act? Has He ever promised and not carried it through?"* (Numbers 23:19 NLT) I ask you, what great things are you believing God for? Ephesians 3:20 (KJV) states, *"Now unto Him that is able to do exceedingly abundantly above all that we ask or think, according to the power that worketh in us."* We have the power of the Holy Spirit working within us to ensure God's promises come to pass in our lives. When we align ourselves with God, He exceeds our greatest expectations.

Not only does it take faith and patience to obtain His promises, but I believe obedience to God's Word is paramount to seeing His blessings manifest in our lives. We see in the 28th chapter of the Book of Deuteronomy; it explains that we receive the blessings of Abraham when we are obedient to the Word of the Lord because we are considered his descendants, "the seed of Abraham," and that when we choose to disobey God, instead of receiving the blessing, a curse will come instead. However, there is a greater promise from the One who is called "Seed of Abraham," Jesus, and according to 2 Peter 1:3-4 (NIV), His divine power has given us everything we need for a godly life through our knowledge of Him who called us by His glory and goodness. Through these (His glory and His goodness), He has given us His very great and precious promises so that through them (His promises), we may participate in the divine nature, having escaped the corruption in the world caused by evil desires.

When pain speaks louder than the promise

But what do you do when pain begins to speak louder and drowns out the promises that have been spoken over you? What do you do when your body is aching, your heart is breaking, your mind is cluttered, and you are discouraged? Sometimes while waiting for a promise to come to fruition, there is a process that we must go through, and that process can be painful. The pain can cause us to forget the promise that God spoke to us when all was going well. But even through the pain, there is always a divine purpose. We must remember no matter what we go through, the promises of God remain. *"And we know that God causes all things to work together for good to those who love God, to those who are called according to His purpose"* (Romans 8:28 NASB).

All of us go through tough times, whether as a believer in Jesus Christ or not. The difference is as a Christian, when you face these challenges, you don't face them alone. The Apostle Paul writes, *"Blessed be the God and Father of our Lord Jesus Christ, the Father of mercies and God of all comfort, who comforts us in all our affliction, so that we may be able to comfort those who are in any affliction, with the comfort with which we ourselves are comforted by God"* (2 Corinthians 1:3-4 ESV). When we go through seasons of great turmoil and pain, we must remember to look at the bigger picture. Trust me, I know this is not always easy to see, but when we don't know what to do, we must lean on the only One who does. God uses our trials so that we would be able to help others who may go through a similar situation. Remember, you also have the Holy Spirit, who is known as the Comforter, who dwells on the inside of you. Jesus tells his disciples, *"But the Comforter, which is the Holy Ghost, whom the Father will send in my name, he shall teach you all things, and bring all things to your remembrance, whatsoever I have said unto you"* John 14:26 (KJV).

As you continue to grow in the Word and prayer, you will realize that the Holy Spirit strengthens and encourages you by reminding you of God's Word. The Holy Spirit reminds you of God's promises in His Word when you are hurting or find yourself in what seems like an impossible situation. He emboldens you when you are afraid, empowers you when you need strength, and encourages you when you feel discouraged. Psalm 103 (NKJV, [NIV]), one of my favorite psalms, illustrates this well. David encourages himself in the Lord by remembering all the good God had done for him. He begins with a shout of praise unto the Lord. "Bless the Lord, O my soul: and all that is within me, bless His holy name." When you bless Him, you are not to forget all the benefits that God extends towards us: He is the One who **forgives** all your iniquities [sins]and **heals** all your diseases, who **redeems** your life from the pit and **crowns** you with love and compassion, the One who **satisfies** your desires with good things so that your youth is **renewed**.

HE HAS

Forgiven you

Healed you

Redeemed you

Crowned you

Satisfied you

Renewed you

Here are some promises from the Bible that I believe will help to encourage you when you may need them the most.

Overwhelmed – *"Cast your burdens on the Lord (release it) and He will sustain and uphold you; He will never allow the righteous to be shaken"* (Psalms 55:22 NASB).

Courage – *"Be strong and courageous. Do not be afraid or terrified because of them, for the Lord your God goes with you; he will never leave you or forsake you"* (Deuteronomy 31:6 NIV).

Brokenness – *"The Lord is near to the broken hearted and saves the crushed in spirit. Many are the afflictions of the righteous, but the Lord delivers them out of them all"* (Psalm 34:18-19 ESV).

Provision – *"But my God shall supply all your needs according to His riches in glory by Christ Jesus"* (Philippians 4:19 KJV).

Healing – *"But He was wounded for our transgressions, he was bruised for our iniquities: the chastisement (punishment) for our peace was upon him; and by his stripes (wounds) we are healed"* (Isaiah 53:5 NKJV).

Anxiety – *"Cast all your anxiety on Him because He cares for you"* (1 Peter 5:7 NIV).

Justice – *"He won't brush aside the bruised and broken. He will be gentle with the weak and feeble, until His victory releases justice"* (Matthew 12:20 TPT).

Assurance – *"And we know that in all things God works for the good of those who love Him, who have been called according to His purpose"* (Romans 8:28 NIV).

Trust – *"Only I can tell you the future before it happens. Everything I plan will come to pass, for I do whatever I wish"* (Isaiah 46:10 NLT).

Fearful – *"Fear not, for I am with you. Be not dismayed, for I am your God. I will strengthen you, I will help you, I will uphold you with My righteous right hand"* (Isaiah 41:10 ESV).

God's Plans – *"For I know the plans I have for you, declares the Lord, plans to prosper you, and not to harm you, plans to give you hope and a future"* (Jeremiah 29:11 NIV).

Clarity – *"Call to me and I will answer you and tell you great and hidden things that you have not known"* (Jeremiah 33:3 ESV).

Suffering – *"After you have suffered for a little while, the God of all grace, who called you to His eternal glory in Christ, will Himself perfect, confirm, strengthen and establish you"* (1 Peter 5:10 NASB).

Purpose – *"As the rain and the snow come down from heaven, and do not return to it without watering the earth and making it bud and flourish, so that it yields seed for the sower and bread for the eater, so is my word that goes out from my mouth: It will not return to me empty, but will accomplish what I desire and achieve the purpose for which I sent it"* (Isaiah 55:10-11 NIV).

These are just a few of the promises that I have written and pinned to my wall of God's promises to continuously remind me of what He has spoken to me in His Word. There are promises that are relevant to every situation or circumstance you go through in life.

I encourage you to find a promise or promises that you can lay hold of in God's Word and memorize them. Surround yourself with His Word so that they become reminders of what He has promised to do in your life. Keep His Word near so that during the most difficult times when the pain is unbearable, or you become discouraged because the wait is so long, or the struggle seems endless, or the enemy tries to come and steal what God has promised you, the Holy Spirit will bring to your remembrance what has been already sealed in your heart. This is how we keep God's promises at the forefront and remain spiritually healthy.

You will keep in perfect peace all who trust in you, all whose thoughts are fixed on you! (Isaiah 26:3 NLT)

A moment to reflect...

TREASURE TROVE V

Genesis 1:1-2
(NIV)

In the beginning God created the heavens and the earth. Now the earth was formless and empty, darkness was over the surface of the deep, and the Spirit of God was hovering over the waters.

Barren To Bountiful

What comes to mind when you hear or see the word "barren?" I am sure it does not conjure up thoughts of fruitful plains or amber waves of grain, but just the opposite. Barren, according to dictionary.com, is defined as incapable of producing offspring or vegetation, unproductive, and unfruitful, a tree or land that cannot produce a harvest. Anything that under normal circumstances should be able to produce more of its kind but is unable to for some reason. However, "bountiful" is defined as large in quantity, abundant and plentiful. When talking about creating something out of nothing, where best to begin than in the book of Genesis when God speaks all of creation into existence by the breath of His mouth, by His spoken Word.

Genesis 1:1-3 (NIV) tells us, In the beginning God created the heavens and the earth. The earth was formless and empty, darkness was over the surface of the deep, and the Spirit of God was hovering over the waters. Picture this, there was the earth, and the earth was barren, empty, and without form. Water covered the earth and on its surface was darkness and chaos, and above the darkness, the Bible says the Spirit of God hovered. Then, God spoke forth light and saw that it was good, and **He separated the light from the darkness**. God spoke light into existence on the **first day**. The chapter continues in Genesis 1:11-13 (NIV) then God said, Let the land produce vegetation: with seed-bearing plants and trees on the land that bear fruit with seed in it, according to their various kinds on the **third day.** Finally, in Genesis 1:26 (NIV), on the **sixth day,** God created mankind in His own image

"So God created mankind in His own image, in the image of God He created them; male and female He created them. And God blessed them [granting them certain authority] and said to them, "Be fruitful, multiply, and fill the earth, subdue it; and rule over the fish of the sea, the birds of the air, and every living thing that moves upon the earth. God said, See, I give you every seed-bearing plant that is upon all the earth, and every tree that has seed-bearing fruit; they shall be yours for food" (Genesis 1:27-29 NIV, [AMP]).

In Genesis 2:5-8 (NIV), the Bible gives more details that no shrub had yet appeared on the earth and no plant had yet sprung up, for the Lord God had not sent rain on the earth, and there was no one to work the ground, but streams came up from the earth and watered the whole surface of the ground. Then the Lord God formed a man from the dust of the ground and breathed into his nostrils the breath of life, and the man became a living being. Now the Lord God had planted a garden in the East, in Eden; and there He put the man He had formed. I find it so amazing how God formed man and breathed into his nostrils His very own breath whereas the rest of creation He spoke into existence. We have the breath *(Ruach)* of God inside us; therefore, every time we speak, our words have creative power. Therefore, it is so crucial that we are careful to watch what is spoken out of our mouths. I encourage you to read the first chapter of Genesis for the full account of creation.

I understand that was a lot to consume, but it is imperative to see that *before* God created the plants, trees, and vegetation, as well as all the creatures who would occupy the earth, including mankind, light was introduced. Light always penetrates the darkness, and God had to separate the light from the darkness. God is a God of order, and He does everything with excellence in mind. In order for a seed to grow and multiply, the Lord made sure that everything necessary for its proper growth and development was in place. Light, water, and then He placed man on the earth to work the soil so that after a period of time, a harvest would be produced from that seed that was sown. It had to be surrounded by an environment that was conducive for its development. God designed it this way so that whether it is a fruit, plant, tree, or mankind God has placed within these a seed with the potential to reproduce like that of its kind. Within every seed, there is the power and potential to produce. So, as the Word of God "seed" is planted in the hearts of people, so shall it produce a harvest. God created man to be fruitful, to bear much fruit for His kingdom.

In John 15:16 (NKJV), Jesus speaks to His disciples and says, "You did not choose me, but I chose you and appointed you that you should go and bear fruit and that your fruit should abide or remain, so that whatever you ask the Father in my name, He may give it to you." Earlier in the chapter, Jesus tells them, "I am the true vine, and my Father is the gardener. Every branch in Me that does not bear fruit He cuts off, while every branch that does bear fruit, He prunes so that it will be even more fruitful. As the branch cannot bear fruit by itself, unless it abides in the vine, neither can you, unless you abide in Me." Here we see the importance of abiding in Christ and how keeping His Word in our hearts helps us do His will and live fruitful lives.

"Not everyone who says to me, Lord, Lord, will enter the kingdom of heaven, but the one who does the will of my father who is in heaven" (Matthew 7:21 NIV).

We must guard His Word that has been planted in our hearts unless the devil will come to take it away (ref. Luke 8:12 NIV). Everything begins in seed form, whether a good or bad seed, and as I have stated before, that seed has the power and potential to produce what it was originally intended to produce. That seed could be a thought, a dream, an idea, a vision, a book, or a business, and if it is a good seed that is planted in fertile soil, with the vital nutrients of faith and the spoken Word of God, it is inevitable that the final product must come to fruition. From one seed comes a bountiful harvest.

Throughout Scripture, there are stories of women who went from "barren" to bountiful. In the first book of the Bible, Genesis, we read about a man named Abram and his wife, Sarai. They were up in age and did not have any children. In Genesis 15 (NIV), Abram had a vision where the Word of the Lord came and told him he would have an heir that would come from his flesh and blood. In verse 6, it says that Abram believed the Lord, and he credited it to him as righteousness. Righteousness because he walked by faith in God and did what was right in the sight of the Lord, believing God would fulfill the promise he made. According to Hebrews 6:13-15 (ESV), God made His promise to Abram, as He had no one greater to swear by; He swore by Himself, saying, "I will surely bless you and multiply you." And so, Abram, after waiting patiently, obtained the promise. In Genesis 17, God appeared to Abram and made a covenant (agreement) with him that if he walked faithfully and remained blameless before him, he would greatly increase his numbers. The Lord said that Abram would be the "father of many nations" and changed his name to

Abraham, and he would make him fruitful. The Lord also said that he must call his wife Sarah instead of Sarai because he will bless her and give him a son by her, and she will be the "mother of nations." God kept his promise, and the following year Sarah bore a son and called him Isaac. God blessed Sarah's womb, and from it came nations. In Genesis 18:14 (NIV), the Lord asked Abraham if anything was too hard for the Lord? Do you see a pattern here? God planted a seed (a promise, a spoken word) by making a promise to Abraham. The Bible goes on to say that Abraham believed the promise. Abraham had to then agree with the Word and put his faith in motion by acting upon the Word that was spoken when God said he had to call his wife Sarah instead of Sarai. It says that Abraham then walked by faith, and God kept His promise, and multiplication and fruitfulness were inevitable. Abraham moved in faith, and it was as if every time he spoke and called his wife Sarah, as God instructed, he was speaking to the seed that was within her which produced the promise.

Hebrews 11:11-12 (NIV) says that by faith, even Sarah, who was past childbearing age, was enabled to bear children because she considered Him faithful who had made the promise. And so from this one man came descendants as numerous as the stars in the sky and as countless as the sand on the seashore. Isaac, the promised son to Abraham and Sarah, would eventually come the "Seed" of Abraham, Jesus (ref. Galatians 3:16 NIV). When Jesus died and was resurrected, He was able to produce more disciples than when He was a solitary person on the earth. We, as His seed, must die to our own selfish ambitions and agendas so that our lives are fruitful. John 12:24 (NIV) states that unless a kernel of wheat falls to the ground and dies, it remains only a single seed. But if it dies, it produces many seeds. I encourage you to read the Book of Genesis if you have not done so already.

We see over and over again where God used women who the Bible says were barren, and caused them to become fruitful, all according to His divine plan. From Abraham and Sarah came Isaac, who went on to marry Rebekah, who was barren, and from her womb came Esau and Jacob. Jacob married Rachel, also barren, and from her womb came Joseph and Benjamin. Joseph, who would go through many tests and trials, whom God would eventually end up promoting to a high position in the house of Pharoah in Egypt so that he could be in a position to provide for his family and the people during a time of famine. Another story worth delving into when you read the Book of Genesis.

Hannah was another woman who the Bible says longed for a son. She prayed to the Lord and made a vow (covenant or agreement) that if He gave her a son, she would dedicate him back to the Lord all the days of his life (ref. 1 Samuel 1 NIV). At the appointed time a year later, she gave birth to Samuel, the prophet who would one day be used by God to anoint (consecrate or set apart for a divine purpose) David, who would eventually become the king of Israel. Another woman who is not named but is known as "the wife of Manoah" birthed Samson, the last judge of Israel, who fought against the Philistines, an enemy of the Israelites. In 2 Kings 4:8-17 (NIV), there is a story of a Shunammite woman who the Lord blessed with a son. Also, Elizabeth, who gave birth to John the Baptist, who was born with the divine assignment to prepare the way for Jesus by preaching in the wilderness of Judea. *"In those days John the Baptist came, preaching in the wilderness of Judea and saying, "Repent, for the kingdom of heaven has come near"* (Matthew 3:1-2 NIV).

As you see, God specializes in using what appears to be "barren" and unfruitful to produce greatness and abundance when you surrender and dedicate the very thing you desire back to Him for His purpose. Is there something you have been longing for? Surrender it. Everything God touches, He multiplies and blesses.

A moment to reflect...

TREASURE TROVE VI

Luke 8:17
(NIV)

For there is nothing hidden that will not be disclosed, and nothing concealed that will not be known or brought out into the open.

Hidden and Unheard

All our life experiences contribute to how we portray ourselves to the world. Are we hiding behind a mask or maybe behind others because we have become afraid? Afraid of rejection or being vulnerable, unable to take risks due to fear of failure or success. Are we just afraid of revealing our authentic selves? As children, we are fearless and trusting until some event or incident occurs, or negative words are spoken over us, or an action is taken towards us that causes us to go from being full of wonder to shrinking back and hiding from who we are created to be, eventually leading us to live a life of settling for less. But is that really living? "The minute you settle for less than you deserve, you get even less than you settled for." - American author and columnist Maureen Dowd

This may not pertain to you, but for many others who can relate, you can identify some turning point in your life that had such a tremendous impact on you that over the course of time, you have seen your light begin to dim slowly. You probably began to accept feelings of inadequacy which led to you buying into some false belief that you are small and insignificant. However, I come to tell you this is a lie from the enemy and could not be farther from the truth. *"For we are God's masterpiece. He has created us anew in*

Christ Jesus, so we can do the good things he planned for us long ago" (Ephesians 2:10 NLT).

"You did not choose me, but I chose you and appointed you so that you might go and bear fruit—fruit that will last—and so that whatever you ask in my name the Father will give you" (John 15:16 NIV). You are chosen, accepted and loved by Him. Just as the devil tried to get Jesus to question his identity by testing him in the wilderness, he also uses the same tactics on us. The Bible tells us in Luke 4:9-12 (NIV) that the devil led Jesus to Jerusalem and had Him stand on the highest point of the temple and said to Him, "If you are the Son of God," throw yourself down from here. The devil goes on to recite Scripture to Jesus, *"For it is written: "He will command His angels concerning you to guard you carefully; they will lift you up in their hands, so that you will not strike your foot against a stone"* (Psalm 91:11 NIV). This is a prime example of how the enemy works. He will try to use the Word of God, but with a twist, and if you don't know the Word for yourself, this is where you can get tripped up. In Luke 4, the devil tried to test the Word by using it against "the Living Word," Jesus. But we see the battle was lost before it began. "Jesus answered, "It is said; 'Do not put the Lord your God to the test'" (Luke 4:12 NIV).

John 1:1(NIV) tells us that in the beginning, was the Word (Jesus) and the Word (Jesus) was with God, and the Word (Jesus) was God. John 1:14 (NIV) goes on to say that the Word became flesh and dwelt among us. Therefore, according to James 4:7 (NIV), it is with the Word, when spoken, that we resist and combat the enemy, and he will flee.

God is all-knowing, the enemy is not, but he does follow our patterns and uses what limited knowledge he has about us to use against us. If he has seen that we have a weakness in a certain area, he will attempt to entrap us by introducing or surrounding us with that temptation. He uses whatever devices or obstacles he can to derail us from fulfilling our divine destiny. Thankfully, we have the Holy Spirit who helps us in these situations if we submit to Him. *"For there is nothing hidden that will not be disclosed, and nothing concealed that will not be revealed or brought out into the open"* (Luke 8:17 NIV). Just as Jesus used the Word, we too are to use the Word, and therefore it is imperative that we know it.

There is a difference between being hidden by God and hiding from God. We can find ourselves hiding from God for many reasons. Maybe we have been caught up in a vicious cycle of sin and have more of an appetite for worldly pleasures than godly treasures. The quicker we acknowledge sin and repent, which means to turn from doing it again, and ask for forgiveness, the quicker we re-establish our relationship with Jesus. (ref. 1 John 1:9). This keeps our line of communication clear and our hearts clean and is vital for our spiritual growth and development. He is a loving Father who is always waiting for our return.

We hide when we allow the spirit of fear to overshadow faith. 2 Timothy 1:7 (KJV), Apostle Paul encourages Timothy when he feared for his life by telling him that God has not given us the spirit of fear, but of power, love, and a sound mind. The phrase "sound mind" stems from the Greek word *Sophroneo*. Rick Renner expounds on this further on renner.org, where he breaks down this word and substitutes it in the Scripture, which then reads this way. "God has not given you a spirit of fear, but of power and of love – He has given you a mind that has been delivered, rescued, revived, salvaged, protected, and brought into a place of safety and security so that it is no longer affected by illogical, unfounded, and absurd thoughts."

The devil loves to introduce thoughts that are opposite of what is in the Bible. Knowing the Word helps us to distinguish between what is truth and what is a lie. When our minds get bombarded with thoughts from satan, 2 Corinthians 10:5 (KJV) reminds us that we are to cast down imaginations and every high thing that would try to exalt itself against the knowledge of God, and we are to take every thought captive and bring it into the obedience of Christ. God has not made us to be fearful, but He has made us "fearfully and wonderfully" according to Psalm 139:14 (NIV). Verse 15 goes on to say, *"My frame was not hidden from you when I was made in the secret place, when I was woven together in the depths of the earth."* To be fearful is to be timid and afraid, but to be "fearfully and wonderfully" made means that we were created so intimately and yet unique in design by God with so much love and care. In other words, you are not a mistake! You were not meant to hide in fear, but as Matthew 5:16 (NASB) states, let your light shine before men, that they may see your good works, and glorify your Father, which is in heaven.

Now, to be hidden by God is when He separates you unto himself for a season and for a reason. During this season, you could find yourself going through tests and trials, all designed for a divine purpose. This is a time when you are kept out of sight, and it may appear as if you aren't going anywhere or doing anything. You may feel "stuck" or stagnant, and you may wonder what God is doing in you and in your life. This is when God is usually doing the most behind the scenes. His purpose is to mature you, strengthen you, and mold you for a divine assignment, a specific task for you to do upon completion of this season. This is also a time when you may find yourself praying and reading the Bible more, all with the sole purpose of drawing nearer to God. We come face to face with the inevitable question, "What do I really believe?" Certain character flaws come to the surface when we are faced with challenges. You may even find yourself in a crisis, whether health-related or some other battle that seems impossible for you to face causing you to depend all the more on our loving Father.

Relationships and friends that you thought were solid start falling away, and all the unnecessary things attached to you and may not have anything to do with your purpose begin to drift away. All your comforts and that which was familiar has now been stripped away, and you find yourself alone. However, you are not alone because God is carrying you through this time in your life, just how He planned it from the very beginning. This is a season where God prunes you, which means He cuts off what is not producing any fruit in your life. That which is dead and lifeless. He cleanses you from all that is unclean so that you reflect more of His character. When you surrender to His loving process, knowing that it would lead to your progress, you begin to hear his voice with clarity and see with a new vision what He has called you to do and who He has created you to become before the foundation of the world. You finally get the revelation that you are now being unveiled or revealed for a greater Kingdom purpose.

Two people in the Bible come to mind when I think of one being hidden by God and one who hid because of fear. First, I will talk about David. David was a shepherd boy, one of the eight sons of Jesse, who didn't know when he was tending the sheep, he was demonstrating a shepherds heart, like the heavenly Father, or when he killed the lion and the bear, he was emulating the Father as protector, which would also help him to defeat Goliath later because he knew the God who delivered him from the lion and the bear would also deliver him from this Philistine giant (ref. 1 Samuel 17:34-36). He was hidden all those years as a little boy, being prepared by God, not knowing that one day, he would be anointed or set apart for a divine purpose by Samuel the Prophet with a horn of oil and appointed king of Israel in front of all his brothers. In other words, he was concealed for a season, only to be revealed for a divine purpose at the appointed time. He would be called a man after God's own heart by Samuel and go on to pen most of the Psalms.

King Saul, in comparison, was also anointed king over Israel by Samuel; however, it was done in private with a flask of oil that the people chose. Unlike David, Saul was not a man after God's heart. According to 1 Samuel 8, he would be a king that would only serve to take from the people as opposed to David, who gave and looked after the people's interests. After Samuel anointed Saul privately, unlike David, who was anointed publicly, when it came time for Saul to be made known to Israel as king, the Bible says in 1 Samuel 10:21-22 (NLT) that he was not to be found because he was hiding amongst the "baggage." Although he stood a head taller than the others, he saw himself as small and insignificant. Because Saul saw himself this way and was not a man after God's heart, he eventually would disobey God by not following His instruction which led to him being removed as king.

In conclusion, Matthew 5:16 states that you need to let your light shine before others so that they may see your good works and glorify your Father, who is in heaven. The time has come for those of us who have been hiding or even hidden for a season to come out of hiding and be heard for the glory of God. When you are about to begin a new endeavor, ask yourself these questions. Will this bless others? Will this advance the Kingdom of God? Will this glorify the Father?

A moment to reflect...

TREASURE TROVE VII

2 Corinthians 10:4
(NIV)

The weapons we fight with are not the weapons of the world. On the contrary, they have divine power to demolish strongholds.

Matthew 16:19
(NIV)

I will give you the keys of the kingdom of heaven; whatever you bind on earth will be bound in heaven, and whatever you loose on earth will be loosed in heaven.

Weapons of Our Warfare Keys to the Kingdom

As previously stated, you are in a war whether you want to be or not. It is not a war fought in the natural, although you might feel its effects in the natural, but a war fought in the spiritual realm. You are spirit, and you have a soul that comprises your mind, will, and emotions, which is housed in a body. The body is the temple of the Holy Spirit (ref. 1 Corinthians 6:19). Our spirit communicates with the Spirit of God, and the Holy Spirit empowers us as we engage in battle. According to Colossians 1:13-14 (NLT), God, the Father, rescued us from the kingdom of darkness and transferred us into the Kingdom of his dear Son, who purchased our freedom and forgave our sins. There are two kingdoms at war, the kingdom of darkness and the Kingdom of God, to which you now belong. We have been given power, authority, spiritual weapons, and access to the King of kings, Jesus. When you accepted Christ as your Lord and Savior, you automatically enlisted as a soldier in the army of the Lord. Every soldier must first go through boot camp or basic military training before facing battle. Unlike in the natural where boot camp just prepares you physically and mentally for war, the daily battles we encounter as Christians prepare us spiritually as we engage the enemy in spiritual warfare. The Bible tells us in Ephesians 6:12 (KJV) that we wrestle not against flesh and blood (each other), but that our war is fought in an unseen realm where there are principalities, powers, rulers of the darkness of this world, and spiritual wickedness in heavenly places. Ephesians 2:2 (ESV) explains that satan, who is our adversary, is also known as the prince of the power of the air. This is where he and his demons operate. Before he was called satan, he was known as lucifer, and he held a high position as the minister of worship amongst the angels in heaven. However, that was not good enough for him because he desired more.

In Isaiah 14:12-14 (NIV), we see he was cast down to earth because sin was found in his heart. The Bible states that he said in his heart, "**I will** ascend to the heavens; **I will** raise my throne above the stars of God; **I will** sit enthroned on the mount of assembly, on the utmost heights of Mount Zaphon. **I will** ascend above the tops of the clouds; **I will** make myself like the Most High." If you notice, each sentence begins with "I will," and just like satan fell, when we begin to think of ourselves more highly than we ought, we can quickly find ourselves knocked down to a place of humility. Proverbs 16:18 (AMP) states that pride goes before destruction and a haughty spirit before a fall. The fall of satan and one-third of the angels that followed him centers around his insatiable desire to acquire all the worship and glory for himself when in fact, he and the other angels were created to give all glory and honor to God only. Revelation 12:7-9 (NIV) tells of the events that took place after satan rebelled against God.

Verse 7 begins with a war that broke out in heaven between Michael and his angels fighting against the dragon and his angels who fought back. But he (the devil) was not strong enough, and they lost their place in heaven. The great dragon was hurled down – that ancient serpent called the devil, or satan, who leads the whole world astray. He and his angels were hurled to the earth. This is who we are at war with; however, the Lord of angel's armies, Jesus, has given us power and authority to overcome all the power of the enemy; so that nothing will be able to harm us.

When Jesus paid the ultimate price on the cross by willingly laying his life down so that we may have life, He stripped satan of his legal right over us by snatching the keys (authority) of the kingdom from him and giving them to us. According to Scripture, Jesus told Peter, one of his disciples, *"I will give you the keys of the Kingdom of heaven; whatever you bind* (forbid) *on earth will be bound in heaven, and whatever you loose* (permit) *on earth will be loosed in heaven"* (Matthew 16:19 NIV emphasis added). In Matthew 18:18 (NIV), Jesus tells us, the church, that we have been given the authority to do the same. After Jesus took the keys and conquered death, He rose from the grave on the third day, defeating satan, and He is now seated at the right hand of the Father. Because we are in Christ and He is in us, we are to remind ourselves that when we pray with the power and authority that has been given to us under the "anointing" of the Holy Spirit, we are fighting from this position and therefore no matter what it appears to look like around us we ultimately win.

Like boot camp, you are provided with and learn about special tactical gear, which, if used properly, is meant to protect you in battle. You are also educated about the various weapons you will have to deploy during combat, in addition to the skills that must be developed. During these exercises, the Drill Sergeant will place you in simulations that are meant to mimic real-life so that when you come against that situation, you will know what to do. However, our spiritual experience is not a simulation; it is real right from the start, and we sharpen our skills as we put what we learn into practice. How will we know we can overcome the obstacles and challenges that are in our way if we do not engage the enemy in battle? How will we know the God we have in us is greater than anything or anyone we come against in this world? (ref. 1 John 4:4 NIV)

The Bible has given us several examples on how to use our weapons to engage in warfare as the Holy Spirit teaches us how to pray and access the spiritual dimension. 2 Corinthians 10:4 (ESV) states that the weapons we fight with are not the weapons of this world (carnal or fleshly), they have divine power to demolish (to pull or tear down) strongholds. A stronghold is a fortified place. It could be used as a place to protect you against the attack of the enemy, like a fort, or it can be used by the enemy to put you into bondage. In Galatians 5:1(NIV), the Word says that Christ has set us free. We are to stand firm, then, and do not let ourselves be burdened again by a yoke of slavery.

When we engage in spiritual warfare, the battle over our soul, we learn how to operate our weapons. We must be prepared for the battle even though the war has already been won by the price that Christ paid on the cross. This war can only be fought from a spiritual position in the spiritual realm with spiritual weaponry. As soldiers in the army of the Lord, we have been given access to an arsenal of weapons.

As believers, we must first know who we are and whose we are. This is considered a vital weapon in the war against the enemy. The reason is if the devil can trick you into thinking you are not who God created you to be by whispering and injecting subtle lies into your mind, he can begin to do what he does best, which is steal, kill, and eventually lead you to your destruction. Therefore, it is imperative to know your identity in Christ Jesus. You are the righteousness of God (made right with God) by placing your faith in Jesus Christ (ref. 2 Corinthians 5:21 NIV). He has placed within us, this earthen vessel, His Spirit, His divine nature, and everything that you and I need to war successfully in the spirit.

Therefore, according to 2 Corinthians 4:8-9 (NLT), although we are pressed on every side by troubles, we are not crushed. We are perplexed but not driven to despair. We are hunted down but never abandoned by God. We may get knocked down, but we are not destroyed. There will be weapons constructed to come against us; however, Isaiah 54:17 (NIV) states that they will not prevail. We can condemn every accusation of the enemy that rises up against us. This is our heritage and our vindication.

The next weapon in our arsenal consists of the armor we are instructed to put on daily. In Ephesians 6:10-17 (NIV), we are told to put on the whole armor of God, so we may be able to stand against the wiles (wicked schemes) of the devil. Then, when the day of evil comes, we can stand our ground and, after we have done everything, remain standing. *But before* we put on the armor, we are told to be strong in the Lord and in His mighty power. Zechariah 4:6 (NIV) states that it is not by our might, nor by our own power, but by the Spirit of the Lord that we strike the enemy and damage the kingdom of darkness.

Stand firm, having girded your waist with the belt of truth; in other words, be prepared to engage the enemy in battle with the knowledge of the truth of God's Word. John 8:32 (KJV) says that you shall know the truth, and the truth shall make you free. Jesus said, *"I am the Way, the Truth, and the Life, no man can come to the Father except through Me"* (John 14:6 NIV). In other words, there is no other way but Jesus, there is no other truth, but Jesus and He is the resurrection and the life. He came to set the captives free.

The next piece of armor we are to put on is the breastplate of righteousness, continuously reminding ourselves who we are in Christ, that we are the righteousness of God in Christ Jesus. It is not by anything you or I have accomplished but by what Christ has finished on the cross. A breastplate covers and protects vital organs like the heart, which according to Proverbs 4:23 (NIV), above all else, you are to guard your heart, for everything you do flows from it, or as another version reads (NLT), it determines the course of your life. Out of the abundance of the heart, the mouth speaks, according to Matthew 12:34 (ESV). Therefore, if we don't guard our hearts, we allow offenses and unforgiveness to seep in and take root, leading to negative words being spoken or actions that wound others and become a stumbling block, hindering our walk with the Lord as well. The enemy knows this and seeks out those he can use to cause harm to others. Therefore, it is imperative that we remember to put on the breastplate of righteousness. *"Death and life are in the power of the tongue; and those who love it shall eat its fruits"* (Proverbs 18:21 ESV). We want to be used by God, not the devil.

We are then told to put on shoes to be ready to spread the Good News that gives peace. Good, durable shoes help provide you with a firm stance when you are getting ready to fight a battle. The devil would love to stop you from spreading the gospel of salvation which brings peace to others. One of the names of God is Jehovah Shalom; the Lord is Peace. So many people in this chaotic world are looking for peace, and because you are a believer in Jesus

Christ, the Peace Giver, Paul tells us to put these shoes on our feet to proclaim the gospel of peace to all those who are in need. "How beautiful are the feet of those who bring good news!" (Romans 10:15 NIV)

Next, we are to take up the shield of faith. Unlike the breastplate that the Roman soldiers wore to protect them, the shield was a weapon they could maneuver in any direction to block the "flaming arrows" that his enemy would launch against him. In his book, *Sparkling Gems*, Rick Renner writes, "Roman soldiers would saturate their shields in water before battle because when their enemy would shoot flaming arrows at them, the water-soaked shield would extinguish the flame, but if they failed to do this, the flame could set the shield on fire, thereby rendering it useless. We are to take up the shield of faith to extinguish every fiery dart of "doubt" the enemy throws our way. The enemy tries to attack your belief system. Your mind is constantly being bombarded with "thoughts," fiery darts of doubt, fear, and lies, from the enemy to bring you into a state of confusion. Faith in the Word of God counteracts all the lies the enemy spews in our direction. Taking up the shield of faith is a powerful weapon that you can use against the enemy because it allows what you believe in to become the very foundation upon which every other belief system is compared and measured. Hebrews 11:1(KJV) says that faith is the **substance** of things hoped for and the **evidence** of things not yet seen. When we stand on the Word of God and believe what it says to be true, it causes us to be victorious in battle.

"Be sober, be vigilant; because your adversary the devil walks about like a roaring lion, seeking whom he may devour" (1 Peter 5:8 NKJV). As you see, he is "like" a roaring lion, but in actuality, he can only be as big and as loud as we allow. What do you really believe

about God? Do you believe He is who He says He is? Do you believe He can do what He says can do? Here you must remind yourself that God can do exceedingly, abundantly above all that you may ask, think, or imagine because His mighty power is at work within you (ref. Ephesians 3:20).

In Ephesians 6:17-18 (NIV), Paul instructs us to take the helmet of salvation **and** the sword of the Spirit, which is the Word of God. And pray in the Spirit on all occasions with all kinds of prayers and requests. Be alert and always keep on praying for all the Lord's people. The function of any helmet is to protect your head. Any strike or blow to the head can lead to a person sustaining a debilitating injury which can lead to them suffering from residual deficits or, worse, death. The enemy would like nothing more than to get you out of the fight.

Paul tells us to take the sword of the Spirit, which is the Word of God. The Word, according to Hebrews 4:12, is alive and active. Sharper than any double-edged sword. The sword that Paul is talking about is not a natural sword that a soldier would strike their opponent with, but a spiritual sword, the sword of the Holy Spirit that we as Christians can wield, destroying our enemy when we speak the Word of God with authority. The Word can do major damage to the kingdom of darkness when we pray.

I see these two weapons (the Word and Salvation) being used in conjunction with each other. We need to constantly remind ourselves that we have the mind of Christ and remember what Christ accomplished on the cross to save us. I believe that as we take the sword which signifies the Word of God and allow the Spirit of God, the Holy Spirit within to wield the Word that comes out of our mouth, the helmet of salvation blocks the enemy from landing any deadly blows. It is so important that we keep our minds covered and protected from the onslaught of negative thoughts the devil throws at us. After someone accepts Christ, the enemy often begins to sow seeds of doubt into the new believer about their salvation. This is the reason I place so much emphasis on reading, meditating, and speaking the Word because the more we speak it, the more we hear it, and transformation begins to take place. In Romans 12:2 (NIV), we are urged to not conform to the patterns of this world but to be transformed by the renewing of our minds. When the enemy comes with thoughts that are contrary to the Word of God, we are to cast these thoughts and imaginations down and take each one captive by bringing them to the obedience of Christ (ref. 2 Corinthians 10:5).

Finally, Paul says that we are to pray in the Spirit on all occasions with all kinds of prayers and requests. Be alert and always keep on praying for all the Lord's people. Not only should we pray for ourselves, but we are to pray for others as well. Philippians 4:6-7 (ESV) states that we should not be anxious or worried about anything. But in everything, by prayer and supplication (the action of asking for something earnestly or humbly), with thanksgiving, let your requests be made known to God. And the peace of God, which surpasses all understanding, will guard your hearts and minds in Christ Jesus. Paul understood the significance and importance of praying for others. In Scripture, we see he, as well as Jesus, prayed for believers. Praying for others is a selfless act that helps to edify the body of Christ. Prayer is essential in a believer's life; it strengthens and encourages us and activates our spiritual weapons, especially when it is coupled with fasting. When we choose to deny our fleshly appetites to seek a deeper, more meaningful relationship with God, He responds by satisfying our deepest longing for more of Him and revealing to us more of His glory. Prayer is to our spirit like air is to our body. Prayer is our lifeline to the Father. It is how we get our instructions on how to proceed strategically against the enemy.

2 Chronicles 20 (NIV) gives us a perfect example of how to engage the enemy in battle. Jehoshaphat, who was the King of Judah, was told that a vast army was coming against him and the people of Judah, and he became alarmed. Jehoshaphat **first Inquired of the Lord**, then **Proclaimed a Fast**, and **Prayed**, and **Sought the Lord**. The Lord reassured him that the battle was not theirs to fight, but His to fight. They were instructed to **take up their positions** and **stand firm** and **see the deliverance of the Lord**. Afterward, the bible says, Jehoshaphat bowed down, and the people fell down in **worship before the Lord**. Early the next morning, Jehoshaphat stood and told the people of Judah to **have faith in the Lord, for He will uphold you**. He appointed men to **sing** and **praise** and **give thanks to the Lord. The Lord then set ambushes against their enemy,** and **the enemy was defeated**. This is so powerful because it was a strategy that the people of God used back then and is still just as effective in the way we wage war today. Although, I have already written about the power of praise and worship, it is worth emphasizing here that the Lord set ambushes against their enemies as they began to sing and praise.

There are two more powerful weapons that the believer has at their disposal when it comes to spiritual warfare: the name of Jesus and the application of His blood. According to John 14:13 (NIV), whatever we ask in Jesus' name, He said He would do so that the Father may be glorified in the Son. His name provides a safe refuge, *"The name of the Lord is a strong tower; The righteous runs into it and is safe"* (Proverbs 18:10 (NASB).

The Bible tells us in Mark 16 (NIV), after Jesus had risen, He appeared to the Eleven disciples and rebuked them for their lack of faith and their stubborn refusal to believe those who had seen him after he had risen. He said to them, *"Go into all the world and preach the gospel to all creation. Whoever believes and is baptized will be saved, but whoever does not believe will be condemned. And these signs will accompany those who believe: **In my name** they will drive out demons; they will speak in new tongues; they will pick up snakes with their hands; and when they drink deadly poison, it will not hurt them at all; they will place their hands on sick people, and they will get well."* Luke 10:17 (NLT) tells of the 72 disciples that Jesus sent to spread the good news, and they returned with joy, saying, "Lord, even the demons obey us when we use your name!" There are several examples of when the Apostles spoke the name of Jesus to cast unclean spirits out of people. *"Therefore God also has highly exalted Him and given Him the name which is above every name, that at the name of Jesus every knee should bow, of those in heaven, and of those on earth, and of those under the earth, and that every tongue should confess that Jesus Christ is Lord, to the glory of God the Father"* (Philippians 2:9-10 NKJV).

I cannot conclude without mentioning a weapon in our arsenal that is extremely potent, which is the blood of Jesus. His blood was the only blood that could be shed to cover our sins once and for all and redeem us back to God. It was the blood of a spotless lamb that the Israelites were told to put on their doorposts so that the Lord would Passover and not allow the destroyer to enter their households thus ensuring their firstborn would be kept safe (ref. Exodus 12:21-23 ESV). When we apply the blood of Jesus to our lives, we are, in essence, saying to the devil we are covered and protected from any of your evil devices, and you have already been defeated. We must plead the blood of Jesus over our minds, bodies, children, homes, and whatever it is that we need to protect. To plead is to present and state a position, and this is what the blood has accomplished for us. It speaks on our behalf and states the fact that the devil has no legal right over us. Because of the blood of Jesus and the word of our testimony, the Bible says we overcome (ref. Revelation 12:11 NIV).

"He [Christ] *did not enter by means of the blood of goats and calves; but he entered the Most Holy Place once for all by his own blood, thus obtaining[a] eternal redemption"* (Hebrews 9:12 NIV emphasis added). The law required everything had to be cleansed with blood, and without the shedding of blood, there could be no forgiveness (ref. Hebrews 9:22 NIV). *"Jesus said, 'Do not think that I have come to abolish the Law or the Prophets; I have not come to abolish them but to fulfill them"* (Matthew 5:17 NIV).

Spiritual Weapons

> Holy Spirit (Power)
> Keys to the Kingdom (Authority)
> Knowing your True Identity in Christ
> Knowing your Position in Christ
> The Full Armor of God
> Prayer
> Praise and Worship
> The Word of God
> The Name of Jesus
> The Blood of Jesus

A moment to reflect...

TREASURE TROVE VIII

1 Corinthians 12:31
(NIV)

Now eagerly desire the greater gifts. And yet I will show you the most excellent way.

Love – The Most Excellent Way!

From birth, we enter the world yearning for comfort and the love of our parents. Even during pregnancy, the unborn baby experiences the emotions and feelings (depression, rejection, etc.) that the mother has, which can have lasting effects on the child well into adulthood. As we become children, we long for acceptance and to feel safe and secure in our surroundings. Many times, if we lack any of these, especially love, it can have a negative impact on us as we become adults. But there is a love that surpasses any human love; it is unconditional and never-ending. A love so extravagant, it reaches higher than the heavens *"For great is your love, higher than the heavens; your faithfulness reaches to the skies"* (Psalm 108:4 NIV).

1 John 3:1 (TPT) says that we should look with wonder at the depth of the Father's marvelous love that He has lavished on us! He has called us and made us His very own beloved children. Yes, we are children of the Most High God, made in His image, and as His children, we are also called to love. Jesus is love, the very essence of who He is. His divine nature encompasses love. *"This is how we know what love is: Jesus Christ laid down His life for us. And we*

ought to lay down our lives for our brothers and sisters; let us not love with words or speech, but with actions and in truth" (1 John 3:16 and 18 NIV).

Writing this book has been what I call a labor of love. I truly believe that there will be people who read this book who may not have opened a bible before, and if that is you, I pray this book leads you on an unforgettable journey to falling in love with Jesus. I can recall when I first came to know Jesus; it was after I finished college. I was at a crossroads in my life. I had no clear direction, and nothing was going according to the plan I had envisioned for my life. I was feeling lost and confused because of a series of events and life experiences that had occurred throughout my life. I felt as though I was wandering, searching for something, but not knowing what. Then one day, I had a divine encounter with a stranger on the train who invited me to audition for a band that was looking for singers. It piqued my curiosity, so my friend and I auditioned, and the next thing I knew, we were singing in a "Christian" band for two years. Isn't God funny? I was singing about a God I didn't know but came to know of His love that drew me even closer to Him, and I quickly fell in love. This encounter changed the trajectory of my life. Within two weeks from joining the band, I started attending a church and was taught the Word of God and how it related to everyday living. I remember thinking to myself, wow, all of that is in the Bible. Every chance I got, I saturated my mind with Scripture. This began a love relationship between the Father and me, so how can I not share this with you. The Word of God changed my life, and if it were not for someone introducing me to Jesus, I would not have been aware that there really is a light that can pierce the darkness. *"We can make our plans, but the Lord determines our steps"* (Proverbs 16:9 NLT).

The Word of God is life-changing and transformational when you apply what is written in it. God's unconditional love changed me, and I know it will do the same for you. 1 John 4:19 (KJV) says that we love Him because He first loved us. We can love each other because the love of the Father is in us. This is how the world would know we are His disciples. *"Your love for one another will prove to the world that you are my disciples"* (John 13:35 NLT). We are the evidence of God's love.

Now that we have covered Who love is let's talk more about **what** love is and what love does. 1 Corinthians 12:31(NIV) tells us that there is a most excellent way, and we find that it is love. You can possess spiritual gifts, but if you don't have love, then you don't have anything. Love is defined in the following passage, *"Love is patient, love is kind. It does not envy, it does not boast, it is not proud. It does not dishonor others, it is not self-seeking, it is not easily angered, it keeps no record of wrongs. Love does not delight in evil but rejoices with the truth. It always protects, always trusts, always hopes, always perseveres. Love never fails..."* (1 Corinthians 13:4-8 NIV). In 1 Peter 4:8 (NIV), we see love covers a multitude of sins. 1 John 4:18 (NIV) tells us that perfect love drives out fear. We are told to love one another, for love comes from God and that everyone who loves has been born of God and knows God. Love also gives, "For God so loved the world that He gave His only begotten Son... (John 3:16 NIV).

Finally, what does love do? According to John 14, love obeys. Jesus says, *"If anyone loves Me, he will obey my teaching; and My Father will love him, and We will come to him and make Our home with him"* (John 14:23 NIV). As a result of us obeying His teaching or keeping His Word, which in essence means doing His will, He promises to reveal Himself. *"Whoever has my commands and keeps them is the one who loves me. The one who loves me will be loved by my Father, and I too will love them and show myself to them"* (John 14:21 NIV). We must not just be a hearer of the Word, but a doer of the Word also, unless we deceive ourselves. *"But be doers of the word, and not hearers only, deceiving yourselves"* (James1:22 NKJV). Where love resides, there is unity, and where the love of God is evident in us, His power is inevitable. Acts 2 says that when the day of Pentecost came, the disciples were of one mind and in one accord all together in one place. Suddenly, the sound of a mighty rushing wind came from heaven and filled the entire house. They saw what seemed to be tongues of fire that separated and came to rest on each of them. All of them were filled with the Holy Spirit and began to speak in other tongues as the Spirit enabled them. We see that love is powerful, especially when we, as believers in Christ, come together with one purpose: to advance the kingdom of God and give Him all the glory.

To sum it up, Jesus is love.

*"Behold, how good and pleasant it is when God's people live together in unity! It is like precious **oil** poured on the head, running down on Aaron's beard, down on the collar of his robe. It is as if the **dew** of Hermon were falling on Mount Zion. For there the Lord bestows his **blessing**, even life forevermore"* (Psalm 133:1-3 NIV).

A moment to reflect...

_____

_____

_____

_____

_____

_____

_____

_____

_____

_____

_____

_____

_____

_____

_____

TREASURE TROVE IX

Luke 9:1
(NIV)

When Jesus had called the Twelve together, he gave them power and authority to drive out all demons and to cure diseases, and he sent them out to proclaim the kingdom of God and to heal the sick.

The Messenger, The Message, The Mission

In Luke 9:1-2 (NIV), Jesus called the Twelve disciples (followers of Christ) together and gave them power and authority to drive out all demons and cure diseases. He then sent them out to proclaim the Kingdom of God and heal the sick. Because we have the Holy Spirit residing in us as believers, we have been given that same power and authority. Just as Jesus sent out the Twelve disciples, so He sends us as His messengers on a mission to deliver the message of the Kingdom of God and spread the gospel to the harvest of souls that need to hear the "Good News." In other words, we have been appointed for a specific assignment and anointed (set apart) to carry it out. Throughout Jesus' ministry, He healed, He delivered, He cast out demons, He performed miracles, signs, and wonders, and preached repentance, telling the people that the Kingdom of God was at hand. God had a plan from the beginning, a plan of redemption, that we would return to the Father through the sacrifice of His Son.

"Jesus also said, "The Kingdom of God is like a farmer who scatters seed on the ground. Night and day, while he's asleep or awake, the seed

sprouts and grows, but he does not understand how it happens. The earth produces the crops on its own. First a leaf blade pushes through, then the heads of wheat are formed, and finally the grain ripens. And as soon as the grain is ready, the farmer comes and harvests it with a sickle, for the harvest time has come" (Mark 4:26-29 NLT).

In Luke 10:2 (ESV), Jesus says that the harvest is plentiful, but there are few laborers. There are so many people all over the world who are searching for hope, and you could be that one person sent to share the gospel and make an impact in their life. An eternal deposit. The Apostle Paul proclaims, *"God has given me the responsibility of serving his church by proclaiming his entire message to you. This message was kept secret for centuries and generations past, but now it has been revealed to God's people. For God wanted them to know that the riches and glory of Christ are for you Gentiles, too. And this is the secret: Christ lives in you. This gives you assurance of sharing His glory."* (Colossians 1:25-27 NLT). Christ is alive in every one of us who believes in Him. We cannot do anything in our own strength. It is the Spirit of God within us, these earthen vessels, that empower us to do the works that Jesus did on the earth. We are followers of Christ, His disciples here on earth, and therefore, we are to emulate what He did throughout His ministry. We have been given this great commission by Jesus, who said, *"...**Go** and make disciples of all nations, baptizing them in the name of the Father and of the Son and of the Holy Spirit, and teaching them to obey everything I have commanded you. And surely, I am with you always, to the very end of the age"* (Matthew 28:17-20 NIV).

How beautiful on the mountains are the feet of those who bring good news, who proclaim peace, who bring good tidings, who proclaim salvation, who say to Zion, "Your God reigns!" (Isaiah 52:7 NIV)

If you haven't noticed already, the world is not as we once knew it. So many changes have occurred, and yet there are still more to come. However, God has a divine purpose for His church (believers), and we are being prepared during these challenging times for what is in store. *"But understand this, that in the last days there will come times of difficulty. For people will be lovers of self, lovers of money, proud, arrogant, abusive, disobedient to their parents, ungrateful, unholy, heartless, unappeasable, slanderous, without self-control, brutal, not loving good, treacherous, reckless, swollen with conceit,* **lovers of pleasure rather than lovers of God,** *having the appearance of godliness, but denying its power. Avoid such people"* (2 Timothy 3:1-5 ESV emphasis added).

However, God says, *"In the last days, I will pour out my Spirit on all people. Your sons and daughters will prophesy, your young men will see visions, your old men will dream dreams"* (Acts 2:17 NIV). God has had a plan from the beginning, a good plan for His people. He already knew the end from the beginning, for He is the Alpha and Omega. The time has come for the church to arise and be the beacon of light to this dark world.

"Arise, shine, for your light has come, and the glory of the Lord has risen upon you. See, darkness covers the earth and thick darkness is over the peoples, but the Lord rises upon you and His glory appears over you" (Isaiah 60:1-2 NIV).

"Let us rejoice and be glad and give Him the glory! For the wedding of the Lamb has come, and His bride has made herself ready" (Revelation 19:7 NIV).

A moment to reflect...

TREASURE TROVE X

Proverbs 2:1-6
(NLT)

1 My child,[a] listen to what I say, and treasure my commands.

2 Tune your ears to wisdom and concentrate on understanding.

3 Cry out for insight, and ask for understanding.

4 Search for them as you would for silver; seek them like hidden treasures.

5 Then you will understand what it means to fear the Lord, and you will gain knowledge of God.

6 For the Lord grants wisdom! From his mouth come knowledge and understanding.

D.R.E.A.M.S.

Don't Relinquish Every Aspiration, Meant for Success!

One may ask, "What is a dream? What are dreams made of? Where do they come from? I would answer this question by stating that a dream is something that you desire to accomplish or a goal you may have had when you were a child that you have not been able to shake.

There are two words that I would like to define.

The first is **RELINQUISH**, which means:

1. To renounce or surrender

2. To give up or put aside

3. To let go or release

The other word is **ASPIRATION**, and this means:

1. A strong desire to achieve success, a longing, purpose, or ambition

2. A goal or desired objective

3. An aim or target

So, if we were to substitute some of these words in the acronym above, we would get; don't give up on your purpose that is meant for success. We should never give up on our dreams. Once our ambitions, desires, and gifts are surrendered or offered to God, it is only then that we begin to see what God wants us to do with them. Therefore, we should not give up on our dreams but surrender them to the One who put them inside of us.

In each of us, there is a gnawing sensation that we are created specifically to fulfill a God-given purpose. God implanted a "dream" inside each of us. For some, it is easy to discover. For others, it may appear to be hidden from view. But like every hidden treasure, it is in the seeking that we uncover strengths, talents, abilities, or gifts that we did not realize were there. The Bible tells us, *"It is the glory of God to conceal things, but the glory of kings is to search things out"* (Proverbs 25:2 ESV). Along this journey of self-discovery, we may find many roadblocks that lead to frustration, but also some memorable achievements that bring great joy.

The Apostle Peter wrote, *"God has given each of you a gift from his great variety of spiritual gifts. Use them well to serve one another"* (1 Peter 4:10 NLT). To think that God saw fit to give each one of us a gift. A dream is like a seed that, when nurtured in the right environment, along with the proper nutrients, can grow into a life-giving source – not just meant for us but the benefit of others. Are you developing those skills that could one day play an instrumental role in seeing your dream become a reality? Are you encouraging yourself with the Word of God, or are you headed for defeat by self-destructive thought patterns? What are you feeding your dream?

Success is different for all of us. For some, it could be the ability to provide for your family. It could be graduating from college, writing a book, or starting a business for others. Whatever your dream is, I would encourage you not to let it go. You may think your dream is too big, but it is not too big for the One who gave it to you. Take it a step further and begin envisioning yourself in that place you would like to be, and let it become part of your vision. Jeremiah 29:11(NIV) points out that God has a plan to prosper you and not to harm you, plans to give you hope and a future. Your dream is part of a bigger picture and a bigger plan. Continue to fuel the fire and stoke the flame of your dream, and you will see that nothing is impossible to those that dare to believe God.

"Jesus said to him, 'If you can believe, all things are possible to him who believes'" (Mark 9:23 NKJV).

My Prayer For You

Father,

Thank you for each person who has read this book. I pray that as they open their heart to seek you, you will reveal yourself to them in such a way they are totally convinced of Your love for them. I pray that their faith will grow stronger every day as they read and meditate on your Word. Meet them at their place of need. As your Word states, you supply all our needs according to Your riches in glory by Christ Jesus. I pray that your hand of favor and blessing be upon them wherever they go. I ask that you deliver them from any bondage or stronghold that may have them bound in the mighty name of Jesus. I plead the blood of Jesus over them to cover and protect them.

I pray the anointing of the Holy Spirit breaks every chain and heals those places that are broken. Lift up a hedge of protection around them that no harm will come near them. I pray that you would strengthen and encourage them as they journey through life. Increase godly wisdom, give them revelation, knowledge, and a greater depth of understanding of your Word. Help them to discern good from evil, right from wrong, and continue to order their steps so that they may walk worthy of the call to which you have called them. May they feel Your love, experience Your presence and encounter the power of the Holy Spirit. Work in them to will and to do of your good pleasure. For what you have begun, you will also complete. In the mighty name of Jesus, I pray all these things. Amen.

Abundant Blessings!

~ Delon

A moment to reflect...

Stay in touch!

Visit my website at www.hiskingdomtreasure.com

Email me at info@hiskingdomtreasure.com

Connect with me on Instagram - TheHiddenTreasureBook22

Made in the USA
Middletown, DE
12 April 2022

63992823R00073